WOMEN EXPLORERS OF THE AIR

Harriet Quimby, Bessie Coleman, Amelia Earhart, Beryl Markham, Jacqueline Cochran

by Margo McLoone

Consultant:
Jacquelyn L. Beyer
Professor of Geography, Emerita
University of Colorado
Colorado Springs, Colorado

CAPSTONE BOOKS

an imprint of Capstone Press
Mankato, Minnesota

Capstone Books are published by Capstone Press
818 North Willow Street, Mankato, Minnesota 56001
http://www.capstone-press.com

Library of Congress Cataloging-in-Publication Data
McLoone, Margo.
     Women explorers of the air: Harriet Quimby, Bessie Coleman, Amelia Earhart,
Beryl Markham, Jacqueline Cochran/by Margo McLoone.
     p. cm.—(Capstone short biographies)
     Includes bibliographical references and index.
     Summary: Summarizes the lives and accomplishments of five women who
were early pioneers in aviation.
     ISBN 0-7368-0310-6
     1. Women air pilots—Biography—Juvenile literature. 2. Cochran,
Jacqueline—Juvenile literature. 3. Coleman, Bessie, 1893–1926—Juvenile
literature. 4. Markham, Beryl—Juvenile literature. 5. Quimby, Harriet,
1875–1912—Juvenile literature. 6. Earhart, Amelia—Juvenile literature.
[1. Air pilots. 2. Women Biography.] I. Title. II. Series.
TL539.M38 2000
629.13'092'2—dc21
[B]   99-18429
                                                                                                              CIP

Editorial Credits

Angela Kaelberer, editor; Timothy Halldin, cover designer; Heather Kindseth,
     illustrator; Heidi Schoof, photo researcher

Photo Credits

Archive Photos, 24, 40
Corbis/Bettmann, 8, 11, 12
Corbis/Bettmann/UPI, 27, 29, 32, 35, 38
Corbis Images, 4, 20
International Stock/Phillip Wallick, 6
Photophile/Mark Keller, cover
Schomburg Center/New York Public Library, 18
Underwood & Underwood/Corbis-Bettmann, 16, 22

TABLE OF CONTENTS

CHAPTER 1

EXPLORERS OF THE AIR

Explorers are people who travel to remote places. Most of these places are far away and have not been visited by many people.

Explorers gather information about the places they visit and the people they meet during their travels. They often take photographs and write about their experiences. These photographs and stories help others learn about people and places all over the world.

Aviation Pioneers

The explorers in this book were pioneers in the field of aviation. Aviation involves the building and flying of aircraft. In 1903, Wilbur and Orville Wright made the first successful airplane flight. Soon, many people flew in airplanes.

In 1902, Wilbur and Orville Wright tested a glider. They made the first successful airplane flight in 1903.

Most early airplanes had open cockpits.

Today, pilots take lessons to learn how to fly airplanes. They earn pilot's licenses. These documents give them official permission to fly. To earn licenses, pilots spend many hours studying flight rules. They also spend many hours flying with experienced pilots before flying an airplane alone. But early pilots had very little training time. This often caused them to have serious accidents.

Challenges and Dangers
Aviation pioneers faced other challenges. Early airplanes were not as strong or safe as the

airplanes built today. Early airplanes did not have the navigation instruments found in today's airplanes. These instruments help pilots fly and land safely. Most early airplanes also had open cockpits. Pilots sit in these areas in the front of airplanes. Pilots could fall to their deaths if airplanes turned over.

Early airplanes often broke down or crashed. Pilots needed to know how to repair their airplanes. They needed to know how to land them safely. Many pilots lost their lives while flying.

The pilots in this book faced another challenge. In the early 1900s, many people believed that women should not fly airplanes. Many flying schools would not accept women. Some manufacturers would not sell airplanes to women.

The women in this book all believed in themselves. Some of them set records for flying long distances. Others set records for flying at great speeds. Still others entertained people by performing daring feats with their airplanes. All of them proved that women could be successful pilots.

CHAPTER 2

HARRIET QUIMBY
1875 – 1912

Harriet Quimby was born May 11, 1875, on a farm in Coldwater, Michigan. Her parents were William and Ursula Quimby. She had one older sister, Kittie. In 1884, the family moved to California.

Quimby's family moved to San Francisco, California, after Quimby finished high school. She became a journalist. She wrote articles for newspapers and magazines.

A Career in New York City

In 1903, Quimby moved to New York City. She took photographs and wrote articles for a magazine called *Leslie's Illustrated Weekly*. She traveled around the world for the magazine.

Harriet Quimby was the first licensed female pilot in the United States.

Quimby wrote articles about places such as Europe, Mexico, and Egypt. She wrote other articles about important issues of the time. These included child labor and women's rights.

Quimby's job allowed her to learn about new inventions. Quimby was one of the first women in the United States to use a camera and a typewriter. She learned to drive a car at a time when few women drove.

Quimby also met many wealthy people who owned airplanes. She wrote many articles about flying for *Leslie's Illustrated Weekly*. Many of the magazine's issues sold out because of Quimby's popular articles on flying.

Learning to Fly

In 1911, Quimby decided to learn to fly an airplane. Quimby had a friend named Mathilde Moisant. Moisant's family owned a flying school on Long Island, New York. This school was one of the few flying schools in the United States that accepted women students. Quimby set a student altitude record when she flew at 220 feet (67 meters). Altitude is the height of an object above the ground.

Quimby earned her pilot's license in 1911.

On August 1, 1911, Quimby earned her pilot's license. She was the first woman in the United States to do this. At the time, there was only one other licensed woman pilot in the world. This woman was Baroness de la Roche of France.

Quimby's Flying Suit
Quimby soon realized that wearing skirts was dangerous for women in open airplanes. The long, wide skirts could fly up and block the pilot's

A tailor designed a special flying outfit for Quimby.

vision. Many women tied their skirts over their legs in order to fly safely. But this was not comfortable.

A tailor designed a special flying outfit for Quimby. The tailor designed a one-piece suit of purple satin cloth. The suit had knee-length pants and a hood. Quimby wore flying goggles, elbow-length gloves, and a long, leather coat with the suit.

Flying Feats

Quimby began to race in air meets after she earned her license. Pilots competed for prize money during these flying contests.

On September 4, 1911, Quimby competed in her first air meet. This meet was at the Richmond County Fair in Staten Island, New York. She flew in front of a crowd of 20,000 people and won $1,500. Later that month, she raced in an air meet in Nassau County, New York. She defeated Helene Dutrieu during that meet. At the time, Dutrieu was France's leading female pilot.

In October 1911, Quimby went to Mexico to perform in a flying exhibition. Pilots show off their flying skills during exhibitions. Quimby's exhibition was part of an inauguration ceremony for Mexico's new president.

An Airplane of Her Own

Quimby continued to learn new flying skills. In France, she learned to fly a monoplane. These airplanes have one set of wings. The biplane was the common plane of that time. Biplanes have two pairs of wings.

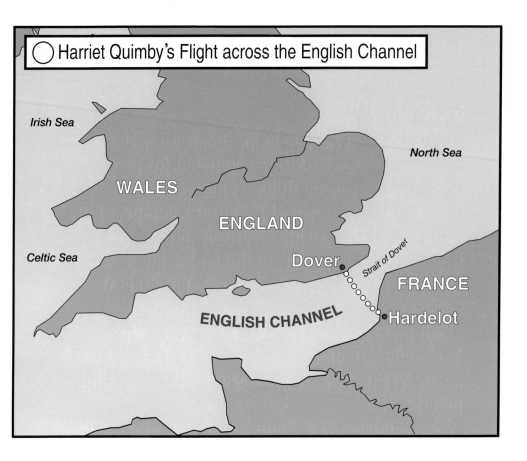

Irish Sea

North Sea

WALES

ENGLAND

Celtic Sea

Dover
Strait of Dover

FRANCE

ENGLISH CHANNEL

Hardelot

Quimby decided she wanted to fly across the English Channel. She wanted to be the first female pilot to cross this body of water between England and France.

On April 16, 1912, Quimby took off in a borrowed airplane from Dover, England. She flew at a height of 1,500 feet (457 meters). She crossed the channel in about one hour. She landed at a beach near Hardelot, France. Many

French people greeted her with gifts. But newspapers paid little attention to Quimby's feat. The newspapers were full of stories about the passenger ship *Titanic*. The ship sank the day before Quimby's flight.

Quimby bought a monoplane in France. She then brought her plane by ship back to the United States.

Honored Pilot

On July 1, 1912, Quimby planned to fly in the Boston Harvard Air Meet near Quincy, Massachusetts. She took the manager of the meet on a short flight before the event. But Quimby had equipment problems during the flight. The plane flipped over. Quimby and the manager were thrown from their seats and killed. The airplane then returned to an upright position. It glided to a safe landing in the water nearby.

Quimby inspired many other pilots. In 1991, the U.S. Postal Service issued a stamp in Quimby's honor. Quimby is pictured on the stamp wearing her purple satin flying suit.

CHAPTER 3

BESSIE COLEMAN
1893 − 1926

Bessie Coleman was born January 26, 1893, in Atlanta, Texas. She was the 12th child in a family of 13 children. Her parents' names were George and Susan Coleman. Her mother was African American and had been born a slave. Her father was part African American and part American Indian.

Difficult Childhood

Coleman's father left the family when Coleman was 7 years old. Coleman's mother was a laundry worker. She washed and ironed clothes for other people.

Coleman's mother did not know how to read. But she wanted her children to have an education. She encouraged them to read and to attend school.

Bessie Coleman was the first African American to earn an international pilot's license.

Coleman earned her pilot's license in France.

Coleman and her brothers and sisters picked cotton to help support their family. Coleman also did laundry work to earn money for college. In 1910, she attended the Colored Agricultural and Normal University in Langston, Oklahoma. But she only could afford to attend college for one year.

In 1915, Coleman moved to Chicago, Illinois. She lived with one of her brothers and attended a beauty school. She trained to be a manicurist. These people care for other people's fingernails and hands. She got a job as a manicurist in a barbershop in Chicago.

Inspired to Fly

Coleman met people at the barbershop who told her stories about flying airplanes. She read about pilot Blanche Stuart Scott. In 1910, Scott became the first woman pilot to fly solo. Pilots fly alone on solo flights. Coleman also read about Harriet Quimby and pilots who flew in World War I (1914–1918). Coleman decided she wanted to learn to fly an airplane.

Coleman applied to several flying schools in the United States. All of these schools refused to admit her. The schools would not accept her because she was African American and a woman. Coleman then met Robert Abbott at the barbershop. Abbott was the founder of an African American newspaper called the *Chicago Defender*. He suggested that Coleman go to France to learn to fly. Female and African American pilots were more accepted in France than in the United States.

Coleman began saving her money for a trip to France. She also attended school at night to learn the French language. In 1919, she sailed to France. But she soon ran out of money. She returned to

Barnstormers traveled from town to town performing stunts in airplanes.

Chicago and took a job as a manager of a chili restaurant. This job paid more than the job in the barbershop. By 1920, she had saved enough money to return to France.

In November 1920, Coleman enrolled in the Aviation School of the Caudron Brothers in Le Cretoy, France. On June 15, 1921, she became the first African American to earn an international pilot's license. This license allowed her to fly throughout the world.

A Career as a Barnstormer

In September 1921, Coleman returned to the United States. She became a barnstormer. These pilots traveled from town to town performing stunts in airplanes.

Coleman performed daring feats in her airplane. She dove and dipped close to the people watching the exhibition. She soared to a height of nearly 1,000 feet (about 300 meters). She also performed parachute jumps out of her airplane while another pilot flew the plane. Parachutes are large pieces of strong, lightweight fabric attached to thin ropes. They allow people to jump from high places and then float slowly and safely to the ground.

Pilots often crashed their planes during the early years of aviation. Many pilots were injured or killed. In 1924, Coleman's plane crashed during an air show in California. She broke several ribs and one of her legs in the accident. The crash forced her to take time off from flying to heal.

In the Air Again

After she was well, Coleman bought an airplane. She bought a used Curtiss JN-4 because she had little money. This airplane had been used in World War I. Pilots nicknamed this plane a "Jenny."

In 1922, Coleman flew at an exhibition in Garden City on Long Island, New York.

Coleman's plane had a hand-turned propeller. These blades on the front of an airplane provide the force to make the plane fly. Coleman had to turn the blades by hand to start the plane.

Coleman planned to use this plane to fly in exhibitions. She hoped to use the money she earned in exhibitions to open a flying school. This school would teach other African American women to fly airplanes.

Coleman's Last Flight

On April 30, 1926, Coleman flew in an exhibition in Jacksonville, Florida. During the flight, a wrench fell into the airplane's control gears and jammed them. The plane turned over. Coleman was not wearing a seat belt. She fell about 2,000 feet (about 600 meters) to her death.

When she died, Coleman had a letter from a 12-year-old girl in her pocket. The letter thanked Coleman for being an inspiration for other African Americans.

Honoring Bessie Coleman

Coleman is buried in Lincoln Cemetery in Chicago. In 1990, government officials in Chicago renamed a road near Chicago's O'Hare Airport "Bessie Coleman Drive." In 1992, Chicago Mayor Richard M. Daley Jr. named May 2 as "Bessie Coleman Day." Each Memorial Day, African American pilots fly their planes over Coleman's grave and drop flowers.

In 1995, the U.S. Postal Service issued a stamp in Coleman's honor. She is pictured on the stamp wearing her aviator's cap and flying goggles.

CHAPTER 4

AMELIA EARHART
1897 – 1937

Amelia Earhart was born July 24, 1897, in
Atchison, Kansas. Her parents were Edwin and
Amy Earhart. She had a younger sister, Muriel.

Early Life

Earhart's father worked as a lawyer for the Rock
Island Railroad. The family moved often because
of his job. Earhart lived in Kansas, Illinois, Iowa,
Minnesota, and Missouri during her childhood.

Earhart attended many different schools
as a child. In 1915, she graduated from Hyde
Park High School in Chicago. A year later, she
attended college at the Ogontz School near
Philadelphia, Pennsylvania.

In 1917, Earhart visited her sister in Toronto,
Ontario, Canada. She stayed in Toronto to work as

**Amelia Earhart is one of the best-known aviators of
all time.**

a nurse's aide in a military hospital. Many of her patients were military pilots. Earhart listened to their stories. She became interested in flying.

Learning to Fly

In 1920, Earhart moved to Los Angeles, California, with her parents. Earhart took flying lessons from a female pilot, Neta Snook. In 1922, Earhart earned her pilot's license. She then bought a yellow Kinner Canary biplane.

Earhart performed in flying shows and exhibitions. In 1922, she set a new woman's altitude record. Earhart's plane climbed 14,000 feet (4,267 meters) into the air before its engine stopped. She restarted the engine and landed the plane safely.

In 1924, Earhart sold her airplane in order to buy a car. She moved to Boston, Massachusetts. She worked as a social worker there. But she still flew in her spare time.

Flying Feats

In 1928, book publisher George Putnam was arranging an airplane flight across the Atlantic Ocean. He wanted a woman to be a passenger on this flight. This woman would be the first to travel

In 1937, Earhart planned her flight around the world.

across the Atlantic Ocean in an airplane. Putnam asked Earhart to be the passenger.

On June 17, 1928, Earhart took off with pilot Wilmer Stultz and mechanic Lou Gordon. They were aboard the Fokker airplane *Friendship*. They flew from Trepassy in Newfoundland, Canada. They landed safely near Burry Port, Wales. The flight lasted 20 hours and 40 minutes. It covered about 2,200 miles (about 3,500 kilometers).

Earhart became famous after this flight. But she wanted more than fame. She wanted to be the first woman to fly solo across the Atlantic Ocean.

Setting Records

In 1931, Earhart married George Putnam. Putnam helped her plan her flight across the Atlantic Ocean.

On May 29, 1932, Earhart took off from Harbour Grace, Newfoundland. She flew her Lockheed Vega airplane through bad weather. She had problems with the airplane's instruments. But she landed safely near Londonderry, Ireland, 13 hours later. She was the first woman to fly solo across the Atlantic Ocean.

Earhart then decided to become the first person to fly nonstop across the Pacific Ocean. Ten pilots had crashed and died while attempting this flight. On January 11, 1935, she flew nonstop across the Pacific Ocean. She flew from Honolulu, Hawaii, to Oakland, California. The trip covered about 2,400 miles (about 3,800 kilometers).

Final Flight

Earhart wanted to set another record. She wanted to be the first person to fly around the world near the equator. The trip would cover more than 27,000 miles (about 43,400 kilometers). Earhart planned to travel from east to west. She knew the prevailing winds during the early spring would

Earhart and navigator Fred Noonan joined Putnam in Miami during Earhart's flight around the world.

help her fly faster. Prevailing winds are winds that blow through the atmosphere during certain times of the year.

On March 17, 1937, Earhart and navigator Harry Manning took off from Oakland. Earhart and Manning flew in a 1935 Lockheed Electra 10E airplane. They reached Honolulu about 16 hours later.

In Hawaii, Earhart's plane crashed as she attempted to take off. She had to bring her plane to Los Angeles by ship for repairs. The repairs were

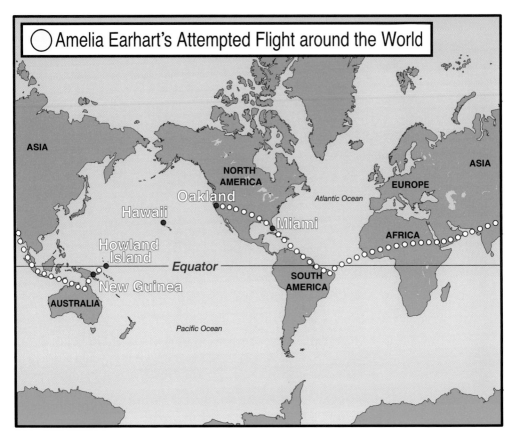

finished in May. By that time, Manning could no longer make the flight. Earhart chose a new navigator. His name was Fred Noonan. The delay also forced Earhart to change her plans. She now had to fly west to east because of changes in the prevailing winds.

On May 21, 1937, Earhart and Noonan took off from Oakland, California. They flew to Tucson, Arizona, and New Orleans, Louisiana. They then flew to Miami, Florida.

On June 1, 1937, Earhart and Noonan flew out of Miami. They flew more than 22,000 miles (about 35,000 kilometers) over the next month.

On July 1, Earhart and Noonan took off from Lae, New Guinea. They were scheduled to stop on Howland Island before returning to the United States. Howland Island is about 2,500 miles (about 4,000 kilometers) northeast of New Guinea. It is about 1.5 square miles (about 4 square kilometers) in area. No people live there.

On July 2, Earhart sent a message to the U.S. Coast Guard at about 8:45 a.m. She said the plane was near the island but was almost out of gas. The Coast Guard could not make contact with her again.

People in ships and airplanes searched the area for more than two weeks. No trace of Earhart, Noonan, or their airplane was ever found.

Remembering Amelia Earhart

Earhart disappeared more than 60 years ago. But people still remember her. Many books, TV shows, and movies have told about her life.

Earhart is still one of the best-known aviators of all time. Today, she remains a role model for both women and men throughout the world.

CHAPTER 5

BERYL MARKHAM
1902 – 1986

Beryl Markham was born Beryl Clutterbuck October 26, 1902, in Ashwell, England. Her parents were Charles and Clara Clutterbuck. She had an older brother, Richard.

Growing Up in Africa

In 1905, the Clutterbuck family moved to Njoro in Kenya, Africa. Soon after, Richard Clutterbuck became ill. In 1906, he and his mother returned to England. Beryl did not see them again until she was an adult.

Beryl Clutterbuck grew up on her father's horse farm. She played with the children of the farm's African workers. Clutterbuck's African friends taught her to hunt with a spear and a bow and arrow. Clutterbuck learned to ride and care

Beryl Markham was the first woman to fly solo across the Atlantic Ocean from England to North America.

33

for her father's horses. She often went with her father to horse races in the city of Nairobi.

In 1913, Clutterbuck's father sent her to the Nairobi European School. But Clutterbuck missed her freedom at the farm. She refused to follow school rules. In 1916, the school asked her to leave. Clutterbuck returned to the farm and never attended school again.

Young Adulthood

In 1919, Clutterbuck married English farmer Alexander Purves in Nairobi. She and her husband settled on a farm near her father's farm. In 1924, Clutterbuck and her husband separated and later divorced. She moved to England but returned to Africa six months later. She began to train and race horses.

In 1927, Clutterbuck married Englishman Mansfield Markham. In 1929, they had a son, Gervase. Soon after, the couple divorced. Gervase went to live with his father's family in England. Beryl Markham remained in Africa.

Learning to Fly

In Kenya, Markham met pilot Tom Black. Markham asked Black to teach her to fly.

On September 4, 1936, Markham took off on her flight across the Atlantic Ocean.

Markham took lessons for 18 months. On July 13, 1931, she earned her pilot's license. Several months later, she flew her first solo flight from Kenya to England. The trip took her about three weeks.

Markham gave up training horses. She became a bush pilot. She flew passengers to remote places in Africa. She also delivered mail to gold mines.

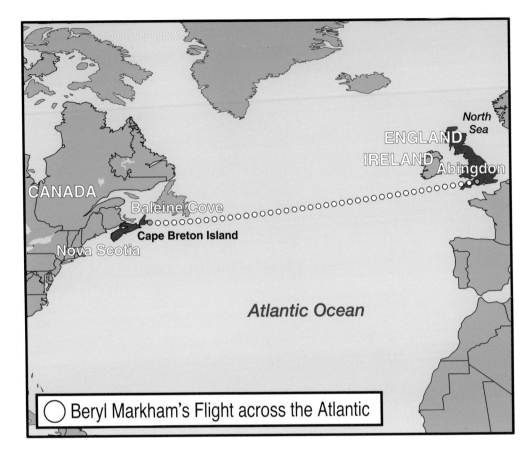

Beryl Markham's Flight across the Atlantic

Across the Atlantic

Many pilots had tried to cross the Atlantic Ocean
from Europe to North America. It was a dangerous
flight. Pilots had to stay awake for more than 24
hours. They also had to fly against the prevailing
winds. At that time, no pilot had flown solo from
England to the United States without stopping.
Also, no woman had flown solo across the Atlantic
from England to the United States. Markham
decided she wanted to be the first to do both.

Markham left Abingdon, England, on September 4, 1936. Her goal was to reach New York City. The weather in Abingdon was foggy and rainy that day. She flew in a new Vega Gull airplane called *Messenger*.

On September 5, the *Messenger*'s fuel ran out. The plane crashed in a swampy field near Baleine Cove on Cape Breton Island. This island is part of Nova Scotia, Canada. Markham had flown 21 hours and 35 minutes. She was only 300 feet (91 meters) from the Atlantic Ocean's shore. Her plane's propeller was torn off. The plane's nose was buried in the swamp. Markham had a cut on her forehead. Otherwise, she was not hurt.

World-Famous Pilot

In 1942, Markham wrote the book *West with the Night*. The book told the story of her flight across the Atlantic Ocean. At the time, few people bought the book. But in 1983, Markham's book was printed again and became popular.

Markham married and divorced again after her flight. She lived in California for several years before returning to Kenya in 1950. She gave up flying to train and race horses in Kenya. Markham died August 4, 1986. She was 83 years old.

CHAPTER 6

JACQUELINE COCHRAN
1910 – 1980

Jacqueline Cochran was born in Florida about 1910. The exact date of her birth is not known. Her parents died when she was about 4 years old. Cochran lived with a foster family after her parents died.

Early Hardships

Cochran's childhood was difficult. Cochran's foster family was poor and lived on the edge of a swamp. Cochran caught fish and stole chickens for food.

Cochran's life improved when she started school. Her first-grade teacher taught her to read and to love books. But Cochran's teacher only

Jacqueline Cochran was the first woman to fly faster than the speed of sound.

Cochran helped form the Women's Airforce Service Pilots (WASPs) during World War II.

taught at the school for two years. Cochran never returned to school after the teacher moved away.

Cochran's foster family moved to Columbus, Georgia, when Cochran was 8. The family found jobs in a cotton mill. These factories make cloth out of cotton fibers. Cochran pushed a cart in the mill. She worked 12 hours a day, six days a week. She earned 6 cents per hour. Her foster parents took most of her pay.

On Her Own

The mill closed when Cochran was about 11. Cochran left her foster family. She got a job working for a family that owned several beauty shops in Columbus. At age 13, she learned to be a beautician. The next year, she found a job at a beauty shop in Montgomery, Alabama.

A customer at the beauty shop encouraged Cochran to be a nurse. Cochran attended a nursing school in Montgomery for three years.

After graduation, Cochran took a nursing job in Bonifay, Florida. This small town had many logging camps where workers who cut trees lived. The workers and their families were poor and often sick. Cochran felt sorry for the people in the camps. She believed there was nothing she could do to improve their lives. She soon quit her job.

Cochran then worked at beauty shops in Florida, Mississippi, and New York. In Miami, Cochran met wealthy businessman Floyd Odlum. Cochran told him about her plans to start a business selling makeup around the country. He suggested that it would be easier to fly around the country than drive.

Learning to Fly

In 1932, Cochran took a six-week vacation. She enrolled in the Roosevelt Flying School on Long Island, New York. Most pilots need three months to earn their licenses. Cochran earned her license in only three weeks.

In 1935, Cochran started her own makeup company in Chicago. The company was called Jacqueline Cochran Cosmetics. In 1936, she married Floyd Odlum.

Flying Races and Breaking Records

In 1938, Cochran became the first woman to win the Bendix International Air Race. This race covered about 2,000 miles (about 3,200 kilometers) from Los Angeles, California, to Cleveland, Ohio.

During World War II (1939–1945), Cochran helped form the Women's Airforce Service Pilots (WASPs). Cochran trained more than 1,000 women to fly airplanes in the war. These pilots did not fly in combat. Instead, they flew training flights and moved planes from one base to another.

On May 18, 1953, Cochran became the first woman to fly faster than the speed of sound. This speed is called Mach 1. It is about 762 miles (1,226 kilometers) per hour. On May 4, 1964, she

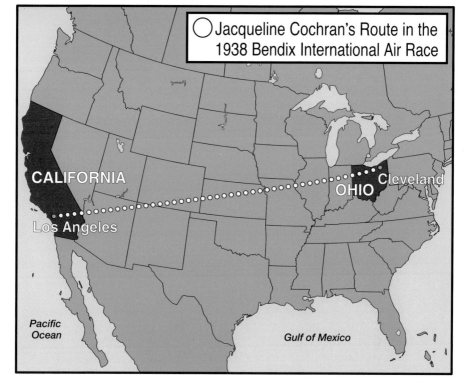

Jacqueline Cochran's Route in the 1938 Bendix International Air Race

CALIFORNIA

Los Angeles

OHIO

Cleveland

Pacific Ocean

Gulf of Mexico

flew at Mach 2. This is twice the speed of sound. Both flights took place over the California desert.

Record Holder

In 1971, Cochran gave up flying because of health problems. On August 9, 1980, Cochran died at her home in California. She was about 70 years old.

During her career, Cochran earned more world aviation records than any other pilot. She won the Clifford Burke Harmon trophy 14 times. The International League of Aviators awards this trophy each year to the world's top woman pilot.

WORDS TO KNOW

altitude (AL-ti-tood)—the height of an object above the ground

aviation (ay-vee-AY-shuhn)—the building and operation of aircraft

biplane (BYE-plane)—an airplane with two pairs of wings

cockpit (KOK-pit)—the area in the front of an airplane where the pilot sits

exhibition (ek-suh-BISH-uhn)—a public display where pilots show off their skills

Mach 1 (MAHK WUHN)—the speed of sound; Mach 1 is measured at approximately 762 miles (1,226 kilometers) per hour.

monoplane (MON-uh-plane)—an airplane with one set of wings

parachute (PA-ruh-shoot)—a large piece of strong, lightweight fabric attached to thin ropes; parachutes allow people jumping from high places to float slowly and safely to the ground.

propeller (pruh-PEL-ur)—a set of rotating blades on the front of an airplane that provide the force to make the airplane fly

TO LEARN MORE

Briggs, Carole S. *At the Controls: Women in Aviation*. Space and Aviation. Minneapolis: Lerner Publications, 1991.

Jones, Stanley P. *African-American Aviators*. Capstone Short Biographies. Mankato, Minn.: Capstone High/Low Books, 1998.

Rosenthal, Marilyn S. and Daniel Freeman. *Amelia Earhart.* A Photo-Illustrated Biography. Mankato, Minn.: Bridgestone Books, 1999.

Van Steenwyk, Elizabeth. *Air Shows: From Barnstormers to Blue Angels.* A First Book. New York: Franklin Watts, 1998.

USEFUL ADDRESSES

National Geographic Society
1145 17th Street NW
Washington, DC 20036-4688

The Ninety-Nines, Inc.
International Headquarters
Box 965
7100 Terminal Drive
Oklahoma City, OK 73159-0965

The Royal Canadian Geographical Society
39 McArthur Avenue
Vanier, ON K1L 8L7
Canada

Smithsonian National Air and Space Museum
Seventh and Independence Avenue SW
Washington, DC 20560

Society of Woman Geographers
415 East Capitol Street SE
Washington, DC 20003

INTERNET SITES

International Women's Air and Space Museum
http://aeroweb.brooklyn.cuny.edu/museums/oh/
iwasm.html

National Geographic Society
http://www.nationalgeographic.com

The Ninety-Nines, Inc.
http://www.ninety-nines.org

The Royal Canadian Geographical Society
http://www.rcgs.org

Smithsonian National Air and Space Museum
http://www.nasm.edu

INDEX

air meet, 13, 15
altitude, 10
aviation, 5, 21

barnstormer, 21
Bendix International
    Air Race, 42
biplane, 13, 26
bush pilot, 35

Cochran, Jacqueline,
    39–43
cockpit, 7
Coleman, Bessie, 17–23
Curtiss JN-4, 21

Earhart, Amelia, 25–31
exhibition, 13, 21, 22,
    23, 26
explorer, 5

Howland Island, 31

International League of
    Aviators, 43

Kenya, 33, 34–35, 37

license, 11, 13, 20, 26,
    35, 42

Mach 1, 42
Markham, Beryl, 33–37
Moisant, Mathilde, 10
monoplane, 13, 15

navigation instruments, 7
Noonan, Fred, 30–31

parachute, 21
prevailing winds, 28–30
propeller, 22, 37
Putnam, George, 26–27, 28

Quimby, Harriet, 9–15

Women's Airforce Service
    Pilots (WASPs), 42
Wright, George and
    Orville, 5